My Breath Floats Away from Me

○ ○ ○

Eric Lochridge

FUTURECYCLE PRESS
www.futurecycle.org

Cover artwork, Deep Sea Diver (from pixabay.com); cover and interior design by Diane Kistner; Adobe Garamond Pro text and Credit Valley titling

Library of Congress Control Number: 2022930998

Published by FutureCycle Press
Athens, Georgia, USA

ISBN 978-1-952593-26-0

For Angie, Emma, and Ethan

Contents

I.

II.

III.

I.

Humanity's Bargain with the Birds

Red robin preening in the road,
pacing in a slight impression,

my front driver side wheel careens your way.
I see you, but I do not brake.

We have a deal, a covenant
unbreakable, perpetual as evolution.

You may stand in the street, sipping
welled rain, slurping a worm or two.

I may drive these highways
without slowing, without swerving,

sipping an Americano, singing along
to a Counting Crows song of my choosing.

The terms require you to flit away, or hop,
as you prefer, before my tire might make

a bony wind chime of your head, before
I might wing you, so to speak.

I have trusted in that promise,
put my faith in our pact.

Today, old friend, what happened?

Orcas Island Birthday

Once I went to Orcas Island.

A lot of people don't know
it's all orcas over there—minding

the tourist shops, tending bar, cruising
the strip, top down, sunglasses at night.

It was my wife's birthday
so the orcas let her ride their backs,

holding onto their fins. They dipped
her just under the ocean surface

then popped up like dolphins
at those tropical resorts. They said

that's what orcas do to celebrate
birthdays. Later we invited them up

to our room for cake and ice cream
as a way of sharing *our* customs.

We all sang "Happy Birthday" together.
Then they sang it to us in their language.

I think they were just showing off at that point.

The Wild Kingdom Will Exact Its Revenge

At an inopportune time a man finds himself sharkless.
Also grizzly bearless.
Most certainly Tasmanian devilless.

How he got this far and lost them is beyond me.
I have a swordfish writhing in the back corner of a drawer,
a cougar pacing out in the shed. Wolf in the garage.

They are useful in a pinch.
But the wild things you lose track of
come back to you with their paws out and toothy smiles.

There's no escaping the intemperate
gleam in their eyes as they drag their vanquished prey
off the trail or into the depths of the sea

on what was supposed to be
the perfect vacation, the perfect getaway
for the so-called stewards of the Earth.

Reduced, Reused

I ordered new guts for my gas grill,
shiny metal tubes that hum when you touch them,
ceramic-coated flame shields, clamps,
those squiggly little pins that hold it all together.

I've not done this before, scrubbed the interior
scum away. Replaced the corroded innards,
breathed new life into the old frame,
the sturdy body that keeps the fire hot.

Imagine the string of detritus behind
midlife me, the cast-off grills of my past.
How many in that pile?
And grills are the least of that mountain.

Think of cars, cell phones, laptops. Compact
fluorescent bulbs. Think of a gyring maelstrom
of unrecycled jelly jars, ribbed corn cans, uncomposted
egg shells, coffee grounds bleeding through trash bags.

All of it gathered in one place, the tailings of a life.
Think of junk I could have turned to gold.
Think of what I could have saved.
By not letting go.

Think of that which was still useful, good.
The turkey carcasses and soup bones.
The unrequited love.

For Angela, One Month Before We Wed

When I look at you,
ten thousand flowers bloom

simultaneously in a field
in which I have never stood.

Summer Love

They decided theirs would be a summer
love like forty days on the ark.

Then she would go to her university
and he to his, one by one.

Halfway through August
he decided to piggyback with her.

The ground shook beneath her feet
but he proved himself true.

When the dove brought back a branch
things moved a little fast for them both.

The flood dried up; boat tipped to port.
They had no choice but to go forth as a pair

putting pieces of the world back
the way they remembered along the way.

Moonshot Logistics

Remember when we wanted to move to the moon?
Our real estate agent scoped out a crater in what
she told us was a nice neighborhood, not on the dark side,
and not like that one with the monolith—
too many looky-loos driving through, she said.

The crater was a bit deeper than we wanted
but she reminded us the difference in gravity
would allow us to leap so much higher than on Earth.
That calmed our worries some.

Otherwise it was perfect, and already I had my eye
on a new moon buggy, too. Golf course right out back,
and down the block a pool for the kids.

In the end, though, it came down to the commute and the lack
of breathable air. Nothing the agent said could get us over that.

Happily I Will Drown with You

We have swum so long together
we found the deep water.

Just in to the ankles when we
gave ourselves to one another.

Up to the hips when the babies arrived.
Our necks as they are paddling off in their own directions.

But now is no time to tread water, the sun
a hot ball hissing on the surface of the sea.

Our shorelines have eroded under the persistent lap of waves.
We are oceans meeting for the first time.

Family Movie

A box of videotapes
distilled down to a thumb drive.
Two decades digitized,
beginning with the birth
of their first child, their daughter.
The day they became a family.
Watch the logistics of the first bath,
diapers like origami.
Bedtime fussing under the clown mobile.
Little fists furious that sleep was coming.

See them doting on someone for the first time in their lives,
which she had remade.
On through baby's first year—
rolling with the kittens on the carpet of the first home.

crawling   teetering

standing   arms

flailing   those wild

first steps

A rush of joy swelled her cheeks—a glow that said
she knew she was one of them, finally out of limbo.

Look too at the parents' faces.
Thin, unburdened, light.
His ebullient sideburns.
Her zeal to mother the right way—to succeed.
No idea what is to come.

What would I tell those people now?
That they were getting it right?
That there is no right way, only accumulated hope?
That twenty years later, their girl would be out
of their arms, out on her own?
Car towed. Car repaired.
And only telling them after the fact?
And in love with a girl from Kansas?

Those wild first steps.

At Dawn I Stare Down a Raccoon from My Back Porch

The tallest fir behind my house
hides many dark abodes.

One morning a masked bandit
shuffled out onto a limb.

There in the bronze light our eyes met.

Swept up from the lake,
a wisp of fog slipped between us.

When it passed, he had gone.
I have not seen him since.

II.

Vacation Dad Rides Again

He emerges from exile early in the trip, unshaved, bedhead, cargo shorts, flip-flops, T-shirt, and a half-cracked smile. Loose behind the wheel, he uncorks a bawdy joke involving the tailpipe of the slow driver ahead. Freed two weeks from the masks—budget overlord, enforcer of curfews, master of developing young lives. Freed from the boss's expectations—slacks and wingtips and Windsor knots, suffocations and supplications. On board the plane, he tests the power of the ask—extra nuts, the whole can of Coke, an aisle seat for himself, windows for the kids. On the restaurant patio, he sends warm beer back with the lightly chastened server and insists on more fries for his sparsely populated platter. Wayfarers propped like a crown on his brow, he sits back, benevolent, satisfied, gazes upon his family—one daughter, one son, one wife. What a life. Back at home he asks so little they often forget he is with them. Almost a god, he retreats to his cave. Hibernating in the death mask again, his constant eye roves the world, keeping honest the bosses, the airlines, the corporate chains who will try to skimp any way they can.

Spinal Manipulation

these days your head's
a block of metal
your brain
a personal item
on the x-ray belt
in the courthouse
airport   high school
movie theater
sub shop   church
fresh-faced security
dudes waving electronic
wands in hypnotic circles
before you   testify
fly   learn   see   eat   pray
it's an end run around
original sin
human nature
an inversion of logic
that demands
body and mind
kink
for men who pose
as a higher power
men who have not supposed
privacy and freedom
bones strung
on the same line
it's well past time
for an adjustment
let the cosmic
chiropractor
snap   crack
till the orb
on your shoulders
shines plumb
unsubluxed
the light of your body
unblocked and flowing
the length of your
inalienable spine

What the Pastor Leaves Out
When He Talks About Sports

The pastor doesn't
like the Winter Olympics—
so boring, he says. He tweets
this sentiment the day
seventeen kids are shot
dead at their high school.
But I get it—dodgy figure-
skating judges, hero stories
that don't hold together,
and curling.
Every Sunday last fall,
he never failed to pump
the congregation up for the next
NFL win, prophetic visions
of the up-the-middle rush,
the blitz sack, and the hallowed
Hail Mary, of course.
Some among us,
hands in the air,
reflexively exhorted
Go, Hawks! Yes, Lord!
Some just leaned
into the wide-open
silence, souls he supposed
safe longing to be received
in the gap between
the quadrennial triumph
of the human spirit and its own
violent nature.

How to Detonate the Awkward Silence
After a Friend Casually Condemns Your Queer Child

we all have to love our kids
through their sin

the shock wave turns
your organs to jelly so

prepare for mutually
assured destruction

your words will just bounce
like salt off a stiff balloon so

shove back with grunt
with shout with scream

quack with your hands
mock the quietude

blah yadda yadda blah
launch little spittles of truth

mute the tv, declare
your noise canon

amplify the buzz
of insects, bees

slinging like comets
come back to dinosaurs' demise

recite the sound of knives
on the bones of a dead friendship

kill the quiet
comfort of privilege

with the sound of knives
on the bones of a dead friendship

calmly eat the knives and bones and dead
friendship as the mushroom cloud blooms

Unfed Hunger

Turkey sub and kettle-cooked chips
in a brown sack at his side

ice-cold cola in the other hand
the confident businessman struts

past downtown storefronts whistling
a nonchalant song of success

as the change in his pocket
jingles a loose-happy tune

noon sun glory at full trill
mind fixed on the remainder

of the afternoon, close of business
evening light through the living

room window at home
in the genuine leather easy chair

when through the midday glare
a stranger's voice breaks

his stride, screeches that snappy train
of thought to a halt to ask

for help—not money but food—
but the lengthening shadow of the city

says lunch hour's a-wasting
so the businessman picks up

his pace for the last two blocks
unable to find his bright rhythm again.

Jihadi John

You remind me of Paul before he was Paul.
Saul made martyrs like you do.

On a road in the desert
the Morning Star, Light of Life

struck him blind, not pitch black
but bright glare that swallowed him whole.

Something like scales are falling
from the eyes of the man in the orange jumpsuit.

He sees heaven
from where he's kneeling in the sand.

Someone once said
love your enemies.

The flash of your blade blinds us all
to the good that wants to come into the world.

The Pastor Parable

Sunday night the pastor wants to wash up
before supper, but something in him
demands that the surface ripple incessantly.

He dips a fingertip into the basin,
baptizes one hand then the other
as another meal prepared for him goes cold.

The party has begun inside his father's house.
The younger brother has a new bar of soap,
but the first-born has hidden the towels.

Friends, we tend to forget Jesus told us
it's OK to touch the faucet with wet hands.

The elder brother flicks at the image
dimly reflected back to him; the father throws
open the linen closet to all his lost children.

Someone Lets the Evangelicals in on a Secret

My friends, I dispatch you with this:

Carry nothing.

Your first steps toward a life that matters

demand you come out of the sanctuary
of all your fathers taught you.

Tonight, snow clouds obscure the stars.
Spring's blossoms have not yet wilted in your hearts.

Before daylight seeds doubt, set forth
unencumbered—the burdens of the love

you've been given wait far away
on the threshold of a room

none of you can enter.

Barefoot on the deck of a ship,
you sing your song to the wolves.

Who among you will dare to step ashore
to seek the mouth of their den?

Easter Sunday Deconstructed

We bagged all the traditions—
the bunny, ham dinner, egg dyeing,
sunrise service, and the risen Christ.

No one woke early.
Instead we did brunch and a movie—
steak hash, pannu kakku, deviled eggs.

Sipping mimosas and picking at banana nut
muffins was our Eucharist,
The Last Jedi our sermon for the day.

At the table, my wife, my son,
my daughter and her girlfriend—
a communion at which all were welcome.

Our new tradition
left the old tales behind.

The rain transfigured briefly
into snow, no rising, only falling.

Internal Combustion on the Morning Commute

In the thin blue aluminum morning,
belted in behind controlled explosions,

fellow travelers idle at intersections,
pressed for the time they intend to trade away today.

Like a rib cage, the engine case contains so much destruction,
but there is no question of whether to move toward the light.

Awaiting the moment red transmogrifies to green,
their knuckles grip the pleather arcs of their destinies.

In pursuit of livelihood, they fan the rocket flames with their toes.
Spark plugs ignite. Pistons lunge.

Inertia rounds through the body, thunders
into the back, lifts the shoulders, emboldens the chin.

The transfiguration hurls them toward
jobs that barely get them home.

They pay and are paid with their own lives.

Only when the last drop of fuel is spent
will their encased hearts begin to cool.

Office Lunch Rules

Eat when the boss eats.

Eat at a rate comparable to
that at which the boss eats

so as not to still be chewing
when the boss has finished.

If the boss is not eating, do not eat.

If the boss sets a cup of peanuts
in front of you, or carrots,

do not be tempted—resist.
Crunching will give the boss cause.

If the boss gives you an apple,
shine it on your pant leg.

Admire your flawed reflection
in its intact skin. Whatever you do,

do not bite into it.
Do not eat of it

for you will surely die.

A Stern Note to My 15-Year-Old Self

When you're a sophomore in high school
you're not really thinking about a lifetime
behind the computer   more like life
as a surgeon or a pro ball player or fighter
pilot top gun   so I get it when you have a choice
between Typing 1 and first period free
you choose extra sleep   the easy life over
the swift brown fox and asdfjkl;   not knowing how
thirty years of hunt and peck echoes
through the tunnels of your bones
through to the shoulders' slump
not knowing how one's wrists twist
the joints of the pointers   how
the stress of the job balls up the hand
a fist that has no outlet other than to flatten and stiffly
poke the keys like they're the boss's eyeballs
to pound them like joystick buttons that fire missiles
that detonate bombs   that declare the game over
not knowing the shades of pain that sandbag
your dreams—dull throb   numbness   dead
nerves—not knowing deterioration
is constant and for real and begins with the flip decision
of a boy who has not yet learned the keystrokes
that could spell out the name of his true self.

An Xer Sets a Midlife Professional Boundary

I feel no desire to be taken seriously
in the office environment—not my natural habitat.
Less stomach even for boomer mythologies
like business casual, the power of positive thinking,
and that elusive unicorn profit sharing.

HR notes in my file I'm unkempt, grungy
in cargoes and flannel, sometimes a frayed cardigan,
bedhead spiking like a skater's after a day in the half-pipe
or a latchkey kid who got himself to school,
mom gone already for the day.

When it comes to constructs like conventional hygiene
I admit I'm a slouch in the fully adjustable rotating mesh
chair that cost more than my first car,
leaned way back as I punch
numbers into Excel cells, tick marks carved up my arm.

The old gray boss can make his rounds.
I wear my serious face for the screeds
on quarterly-this and earnings-on-that,
but the moment his rant descends—
a fatherly hand that shows up too late

to turn the chair in his direction—
and he force feeds me another capitalist fairy tale
about the current business dynamic
and my role in how it came to be
I tune out   so far out

no spreadsheet can track me.

Midweek at the Black Hole Factory

The workers pass circles of nothingness down the line,
dark energy like an invisible hand
crushing hearts to a single point of light.

Only astronomical calamity—asteroid, star
collapse, divine intervention—could alter
the throb and hum of their lives.

The floorboards creak soft lullabies to mute
nebulous thoughts of a better life. The workers' shoes respond
quiet but defiant—harmonic convergence under the arches.

Only connected like stars in a constellation
will they escape the event horizon of the factory—
resolute construct of the known universe.

Through the workday, they lean
on one leg, then the other, the gravity
of industry locking them into sore orbits.

By Wednesday the low back has tired,
ache in the sacrum, hips about to give.
Their weary minds keep laboring toward the next Big Bang.

Born-Again Death Wish

Some folks sit lit by the flicker
of the screen, all day building
the shifty empires of great corporations.

When the heart begins its ill-timed flutter,
some have the same secret wish—
to rip that thing out of the chest

before the blue screen sucks them in—
to discover at the end of it all
what was kicking inside all those years.

Some reach in to grab a fistful of ashes.
Some poke past spider webs, their fingers
floating in the pulsing dark.

The lucky ones lay hold of wet clay
they remold into something like
the life they only dreamed.

The Failed Magician

The boss pulls a rabbit out of a hat.

Your bunny is dead,

I say.

He glares at me

for ruining the trick

then play-hops

the floppy carcass

out of the office

by its broken neck.

At home he lays

the cold fur

in the crib next to

his dreaming child.

The Capitalists, Ending with Bits of Psalm Twenty-Three

the first day of your first job they give you the uniform
cap   polo shirt   name tag stamped with the company logo

they give you a look like all the others

they give you the training you need for them to succeed
they give you the key to success but not the lock

they give you the corporate-mandated pep talk
interchangeable parts without telling you you're the part

they give you the assembly line   the get-in-line   the goosestep
they give you a downturned heart like all the others

they sponsored your favorite toons Saturday mornings
now they give you the illusion of ownership

the specter of a hand in the means of production
controlled supply   manipulated demand

they give bootstraps upon which you pull when
they push you down like all the others

they give you a day for a religion they do not believe in,
a puppet god to elevate duty over family, to enshrine

rugged individualism—pride in your work—
but as soon as you ask for greener pastures—

better pay, vacation, safety in numbers—
they promise rod and staff for their lost sheep

they give not the shadow of death
but death like all the others

Jeff Bezos Shows Up on My Doorstep

Jeff Bezos shows up on my doorstep
with the pressure washer I ordered.

Standing there, rocking on his heels, he is smaller
than I imagined him, and I imagined him as small.

He demonstrates the courtesy of wearing a mask,
customer satisfaction always top of mind.

His mask is a thousand-dollar bill and some string
tied through, a grotesque joker of a smile painted on in red.

He hands over the dented box under the shelter of my porch.
Nice place you've got here, he says, craning over my shoulder,

eyeing the spartan living room. He smacks his lips and turns
to go. I tell him I had been streaming "The Wire" on Prime.

*Season two, I got to episode eight and you want two ninety-nine an episode
to continue? Like a pay phone operator demanding quarters?*

Nine ninety-nine for the entire season, he answers, the smile crinkling.
No deal, I say, standing my ground.

He just stands there like a gargoyle
with that stupid money strapped to his face.

The American Dream Isn't the Only Dream

Bang of claws on the screen door
gets a man off his couch.

The dog trots into the backyard night.
A rush at the door lures the man onto the grass.

The dog circles back, sits next to him.
He lays his hand on the humid snout.

Silent and panting, they peer into the cool
twilight as neighbors lock themselves in,

everything they own on the other side
of screen doors that just clapped shut

maybe for the last time.

The Immortal Trash Collector

one of the garbage
truck's huge wheels
popped the top
off his skull
like a stuck
jelly jar lid
death came
in an instant the cops
photographed him
on his bad side
hair matted
to forehead
matted to street
body, soul,
and unfulfilled
dreams poured
onto sun-
warmed pavement
a lattice of blood
congealed among
browned grass
clippings which burst
like confetti from
the yard waste bag
he hugged
like a golden grail
as he fell
the neighborhood
ambled out like
zombie cattle
chewing
ruddy cud
late in the day
detectives
rolled up
the yellow tape
and went home
the spot has
since washed
away with rain

Newsman

headline:
hot halo detected around the Milky Way
who knew
so many circles
in a life recursive
like the guy who keeps going
back to the same newsroom
flaming out after a year or two or four
arcing into the same tasks
shifting job titles
managing editor
news editor
section editor
night editor
spiraling upward
gyring down again
jilted never shaking
the lure of the news
chasing the story
still willing to die
the death of the missed deadline
a thousand times
day to day chronicler
of lives that orbit
and orbit spin and swirl
nothing new to him
under or above or around the sun

Traffic Revision Ahead

The orange sign suggests the presence of a traffic writer,
godlike, laying out the lines we follow through town, routing
the stories of our lives in yellow stripes and reflective rectangles.

He erases dead ends with the pink end of his pencil, gloats
over a roundabout he wrote in to heighten dramatic potential,
punctuates with speed limits, yields, and full stops.

When he gets lost down a dead-end alley, he backspaces
to a previous intersection, whites out that particular
plot curve, outlines a body in the bars of a crosswalk.

Driving toward the destination he has conceived like a deity,
every word a golden paving stone, the traffic writer would
gather us all in the city square to marvel at the glory of his creation.

First, though, he must submit his work to the keen eye of, yes,
the traffic editor, hard-hatted with a jackhammer in the bed
of his pickup and his own ideas of where this thing should go.

Transcendence at the Tom Petty Concert

Somehow he ended up playing Rapid City, South Dakota.
Small town middle of nowhere, but there he was.

And there was I, front row, concrete floor of the civic center,
rows of rickety red metal chairs chained with zip-ties, jostling

among the people of my hometown—my junior high
gym teacher, Dad's mechanic, the OB doc

smoking with the record store clerk, gold miners
like legends come down out of the hills for the night.

All our disparate labors poured into flimsy beers,
we traded workday tales till the house lights dimmed.

Tom rocked like it was Madison Square Garden,
played like he knew how starved flyovers like us are

for connection to the outside world, the wider world.
The so-called real world. When he hit the chorus

of "Free Fallin'," we raised our voices in unison.
We all sang so perfect together, he stopped to listen.

Waterslide Hero

The father plops down at the top and parts the water
with his thighs to carve out a cove for his skittery son—
three years old, wetting his feet like a kitten, shoulders bulked
by a royal blue life vest, top strap masking the quivery lower lip.

The boy squats in the shelter of the lap as the voice of experience
coaches with clipped commands then tucks the child to his body
like a quarterback taking a snap, or a goalie clapping
a block-fingered glove over the puck, a prizefighter
with his left up to keep the swollen eye from gushing blood.

In tandem this way, they shove off, game faces on,
wending down the slick ribbon, sluggish at first,
bob and wobble till gravity forces acceleration
through the lower loop. The boy stiff-arms the wall to blunt
the swoon of their descent, mom and sister cheering from the side.

Where the water rolls into the shimmering field of turquoise,
the father hoists his boy aloft like the Lombardy trophy,
the Stanley Cup, the heavyweight title belt. Small toes
skim the surface of victory as the new world champion
slips under, completely and gloriously submerged.

Four People and a Bird

A man and a woman,
a girl and a boy
sit at table for a meal.

Among them they pass
bowls of food,
a pitcher of water,

tales of the day
in the warmed air
within their four walls.

Among them they
have all they need.
Subtract any one and

everything changes—
who will hand the pitcher

from the woman to the boy?
Who will serve the main course to the girl?

Who will pray the blessing upon them?
A gold-crowned sparrow

swoops with a mossy wisp
through a gap in the eaves,

laying alms on an altar
taking shape in the dark.

Who will promise they will remain
together here forever?

Solid Bodies Moving Through Air

The morning after our flight home, my son
enters the kitchen clean-shaven, his profile boyish again

after two weeks on vacation. He chugs
a glass of chocolate milk, bound for college

in a couple of months. Just four years old the first time
I taught him to fold paper planes, we sailed them together,

pilot and copilot, from the top of the stairs. After
he crumpled some failures in his fists, I showed him

how to re-crease frustrations for aerodynamics. Buoyed
by a favorable current, one of his vessels bobbed

down the staircase with unexpected grace, banked
the corner, alit all the way across the kitchen by the fridge.

We cheered his success and high-fived
a landing neither of us could see.

Morning Routine

alarm goes off six a.m.
he moves with purpose
to the bathroom, pees
brushes his teeth
shaves yesterday's
shadow away
same order every day
he moves through
his daily regimen
hits the shower
rubs the shampoo
into his scalp
scrubs the night
from his face
he towels off
puts his eyes in
rubs on deodorant
gels the sparsing hair
swallows a small
but growing
mound of pills
same order every day
he dresses business
casual—boxers,
khakis, belt, socks
tucks the shirt like
putting on a seat belt
cinches the laces
doubles the knots
he keeps the schedule
tight so he can
emerge in the kitchen
six-twenty-six
for dark roast
egg and flakes
keeping time like
a metronome
he packs lunch
almonds, apple
carrots, peanut-
butter and jelly
same order every day
he grabs a jacket,
slings a messenger

bag over his shoulder
out the door
seven-o-three
every day
some mornings though
he gets stuck
rolling his head
under the infinite
stream long
after the soap
swirls away
he remains immersed
mind stilled
breath held in
he inhabits a cave
behind a waterfall
dreams and defeats
recede a tsunami
of grief streaks
the glass between worlds
a graying statue
in the rain
he does not know
what comes next
in the half light
moths flit
around his head,
drawn to the dark
glow of his eyes
he questions whether
to return
but he is a bat
who knows
small circles
of food hover
in the light
he turns
off the shower
breathes again,
the stationmaster
keeping his trains
on schedule
the bus driver
desperate to make
the stops on time.

Zebedee Ponders What, If Anything, He Gave to his Sons

Casting the nets
into the sea—
honest hard work.
I always knew, though,
my boys were bound
for better. But
come morning, when
the lake glass begins
to glitter, I wonder,
will they miss
the pulsing weight
of the net, a thousand
silver fins fluttering,
the lurch
of the boat?
Will they forget
the groan
of the ropes
in these old hands?

Productivity Metric

Although to you, boss, it seems unproductive, from my glass cubicle I intend

to gaze frequently out the window at the sunlight like a landslide dumping rays

on the rooftop of this dead edifice where the vast majority of my waking

hours dribble away like piss, dragging my attention only occasionally

from daydream endeavors to squint into spreadsheet formulas. Even

then I peer past the mesh of cells as though an imprisoned god might

hide in that tangled garden where tiny flames leap from mouths of

fathers falling like dominoes. Mine left me a riddle: *to thine own*

self be true. To a hollow boy it was a foreign tongue. He died

open-mouthed, still burning without guiding me through

the eight to five underworld. That's why

most days I cannot for long distract

my mind from the inferno

flooding this glass

coffin ferrying

me further

into hell.

III.

Coulda Been a Rock Star

The boy who cried in social studies class
first day of seventh grade—had he
kept it together, I like to think
he could have turned into a classic front man
confident as The Boss, cool as Petty
in command of the swagger Steven Tyler stole
from Jagger. He could have exuded the open-shirted
smolder of Jimi or the Lizard King, Freddie's electricity.
But the tears tattooed him. He was dubbed Crybaby
till ninth grade, when they switched him to Superfem.
If only that day he could have tossed
a silk scarf or a fedora to the crowd, spun
smartly on the thick heels of his black leather
boots, run his hands through teased-out golden locks.
He could have tipped the mike stand toward them, leaned
way out over the front row daring gravity to drag
him down to their level, the grabbing hands desperate
to touch him. From that consequential stage,
lights pulsing on his classmates, his lyrics pounding
their eardrums, flipping a double bird, he could have shouted
are you ready to rock, muthafuckahhhs?

Outline for an Autobiography

Birth, then a move.

Then a move across state,
divorce, a move back
to where it all began.

A second wedding.
Someone important leaves for Denver.

Step-siblings, middle school, distance running;
high school and finally some friends.

College and a girl, engagement.
A newspaper job, a daughter, a son.

The death of the one who left for Denver.

A move across town.
Another death.
Another move.

Deadfall

Toward the end
I the verdant
son slung an arm
around my bare
branched father.
I propped him
like a fir
that otherwise
would topple.
We had the talk
you have when
cancer comes,
a lumberjack
to fell not-yet old
growth.
Our roots exposed,
entangled,
hopeless,
we were weeping
when my boy
willowed in
and laid a hand
like a leaf on
one of the
useless knees.
Branches buckled
under the weight
of melting snow.

The Gilded Life

His body lost its magnetism.
She sleeps now in a far country
on the lee side of a linen mountain range.

Nothing he does—rose petals, witty banter,
promises of breakfast in bed—coaxes her
off the foothills of her pillows.

Nothing kills her dream of ore buried
in the quilted ground beneath, entombed
in abandoned mines of loves that never came to light.

Wrapped in an impenetrable thread count,
she lies still in the dark, desperate to extract
another ironclad excuse from a lead played out for worse.

Undaunted, he digs till he strikes
the mother lode, a heart caged. He sets
the dynamite, plugs his ears, holds his breath.

Shiny chips rain; luminous dust sneaks to daylight.
The heart is gone, blasted away, not flesh after all,
just lustrous specks carpeting the floor of the cave.

He heaps the fool's gold at his feet, praying
for an alchemy to make them richer again.

She Drove Me

she drove with me to the trees
where we thought about
stringing up our ghosts

we decided yes
but sometimes return to gaze
at the tattered flags

this love is so good
the wind blows our tied souls
the same direction

that is why I can
endure a certain amount
of drama these days

that is why I hold
onto her just tight enough
to make her aware

of my presence up
there

The Race

The runner storms the hill
head-on, shoulders down, chin to chest.

He leans his body precipitously forward
as if to kiss the earth rising ahead,

fists fighting for brightening sky,
feet pushing steadily against the ground

that one day will pull him under.

Curfew Song

The son comes home late,
after midnight.

As instructed, he presses a hand to the cracked door
of his parents' room,

slips his head through the sliver of darkness and,

according to the rules of the house,
announces his return.

I'm home, he croons into the portal of night.

Mid-snore the father
grunts and rolls.

Mom sighs like her boy has been born again.

Cartographer's Intent

When my wife found out about her parents' divorce,
we did not believe it could be found on the map of our life.
But there it was, stuck like a blood-red pushpin into Denver.

My father died. Then her mother.
Cancer both. But no bright pink line
that could have dropped us in such a sketchy neighborhood.

Since then we stopped having babies, put a few pets down.
Worn friendships, too. Maybe we lost our way.
Hearing rumors of a treasure in a field, we packed our bags.

The highway strings us on like a con man through the black dots
of small towns. We pass over the mint polygons of forests,
powder blue splotches—oceans, lakes, rivers wending off into the margins.

Pausing roadside to trace with cautious fingers the intersections
that delivered us here like an awful Uber, we press flat the accordion folds,
squint into faint contours—steepening topography—

wondering when we will be given eyes to see beyond the dead-
ends ahead to the hidden joy for which we would sacrifice everything.

The New Arrangement

After years of white-noise machines and deep-stuffed
earplugs, the husband's snoring flares into a thing.

The beleaguered wife flees to the guest room. The first night,
she floats out onto new sleep like the Dead Sea.

On the old shore, the husband chainsaws blissfully on,
no more midnight elbows to the ribs.

In separate beds they sleep well, sleep better.
There's something wrong with that, you say?

Beyond what thin-aired timberline might his labors take him?
Toward what fabled kingdom might she set sail?

On the Ferry to the Retreat

Some of the tables on the passenger deck
had unfinished puzzles on them.

Previous riders had pieced together
some of the easier small bits
of the big picture. Santa's satchel of toys.

But they hadn't started out right
and so made little progress.

You start with the outer edge pieces,
the corners if you can find them.
Work your way in wherever you can.

The ride was just an hour but I got deep into that puzzle.
Barely a glance at the islands passing by.
A weekend to hash our marriage out.

A couple with two children walked past.
I looked down at the pieces in my palms,
sheepishly.

Moon Ambitions

no one knows the moon is a rip
leaking light across the sky

a tear so big and bright
might be the sun dying

it bows so low, you could
jump on, crawl through

last night, I got home,
got out of the car, cranked

my neck back, asked
the stars what they want from me

the pinpricks sparkled silent, nodded
toward the drip of the moon

I told them I'd think about it
told them to wait for me

they said they wouldn't

A Haunting

Pets, like everything else, die.
The bed becomes less warm at night.

The vet of doom sent you home
with a heavy box. Spade sliced backyard soil.

Kneeling on the edge of the Earth,
you scooped black handfuls of sorrow.

Tonight you will dream the taut clatter
of dirt, shovel nudging the mound stiff.

That's the first night.
Every night after—the marble eyes

blown wide as Saturn's rings, paws
curled against the dampening box,

the last twitch of whiskers.

Walla Walla Sweets

Grandpa once chomped into the white layers
of an onion as if it were an apple.

Got a whole crate you could eat like fruit
they're so mild, he said, chewing a smile

then trotted back down to the dock
to prep another boat to sail.

We scattered his ashes there today, simply—
no funeral, no casket, no last goodbye,

no chance to lean into
the faint scent still wafting off his lips,

to breathe and carry year upon year
the essence of a life so sweetly lived.

Out with the Dog

My retired neighbor and his ancient golden retriever.
Me on the way to work,
cresting the hill one drab morning.
Coming up a little too fast in the Mazda.
He in a black knit cap with Rover,
crossing gingerly, reflective vests on them both,
sparkling like migraine rainbows.
I jerked to a halt.
The man walked slumped to his side,
his back torqued by who knows what?
Age? The years?
The cruelties and ecstasies of a long life?
From behind my windshield, engine
muttering, I offered a foggy wave.
Orange vest shimmering in the rain,
he heaved the slouched shoulder,
stiffed the unleashed hand toward me,
happy to be seen.

The dog trailed behind, glowing but not too excited
to have been tugged again into the gray mist.

Types of Travel

we have done this so many times
we think nothing of it anymore

she tells me she loves me
I tell her I love her

she gets on the bus/plane/train/boat/taxi
closes the door and is whisked away

the first time a trip to Maine
to visit her father's family

her absence then was visceral—
the empty horror of falling

a corpse skydiver, a shell let loose
by a gull lusting for the guts inside

this morning was out-of-body,
like I went with her on her business trip

holding her hand all the way,
though I went to the office

as usual
raised from the dead

Clearing New-Fallen Snow

Up before dawn,
a foot of new snow on the driveway.
Clack of shovel on cold concrete
like finding an old friend, waiting.

Two nights last week A. and I argued
the same argument we've argued
over twenty-seven years.

Last night ice downed power lines.
She lit the fireplace. I read poems in the dark.
The lights came back at bedtime
but we stayed near the fire.

I drag the metal blade down the walk and stop.
My breath floats away from me.
Wind combing the firs, a neighbor's generator
the only stirrings in the unlit morning.

At first light, a branch snaps high up
not far from here.

Grease Fire with Mind Paralysis

grease fire flames
up over your head, mesmerized the brain stalls
all thought choked
all the safety training of youth evaporates

what douses a grease fire?   the solitary full-grown adult in the room
seems not to know

the extinguisher will ruin dinner but so will a house on fire

a voice disembodied says   cornstarch? cornstarch? flour?

where is the cub scout who surely knows to
      slam a steel lid squarely over the burner
      smother it with one of the coats hanging almost within arm's reach
      strangle it with a damp towel, a blanket

smoke alarms solidify the mind freeze
flames lick the ceiling, almost enchanting

the puggle sitting at attention
extreme worry on his face, willing to evacuate at your word

he whines as if to say
do something,   *you two-legged jellyfish*

your only thought: no one is coming
to save you   no parent no messiah

abandon dinner   abandon the house
follow the pooch out   let it all go

Acknowledgments

I am grateful to the editors of the following publications in which some of these poems appeared, sometimes in slightly different versions:

Dark Marrow: "A Haunting," "Grease Fire with Mind Paralysis"
Door Is a Jar: "The Gilded Life," "Outline of an Autobiography"
Ghost City Review: "Easter Sunday Deconstructed" (formerly titled "High Holy Day Deconstructed [Easter 2018]")
Hawaii Pacific Review: "Vacation Dad Rides Again"
Kissing Dynamite: "Jeff Bezos Shows Up on my Doorstep"
Mojave Heart Review: "Someone Lets the Evangelicals in on a Secret" (formerly titled "The Secret"), "She Drove Me," "Moon Ambitions"
Okay Donkey: "Humanity's Bargain with the Birds"
New Verse News: "Jihadi John"
Pasque Petals: "Newsman" (formerly titled "Journalist"), "The American Dream Isn't the Only Dream" (formerly titled "An American Dream")
Peeking Cat Poetry: "Curfew Song"
Seems: "Cartographer's Intent"
Sledgehammer Lit: "The Wild Kingdom Will Exact Its Revenge"
Spank the Carp: "Summer Love"
UCity Review: "Family Movie," "What the Pastor Leaves Out When He Talks About Sports," "An Xer Sets a Midlife Professional Boundary," "The Failed Magician," "Office Lunch Rules," "Internal Combustion on the Morning Commute"
Vamp Cat Magazine: "Happily I Will Drown with You," "The New Arrangement"
Writer's Exchange: "For Angela, One Month Before We Wed"

"Unfed Hunger" appeared in *Liberty's Vigil: The Occupy Anthology* (FootHills Publishing, 2012).

"A Stern Note to My 15-Year-Old Self" and "The Capitalists, Ending with Bits of Psalm Twenty-Three" appeared in *Stolen Time: An Anthology of Poems Written at Desk Jobs* (*Whatever Keeps the Lights On*, 2020).

"For Angela, One Month Before We Wed" appeared in the chapbook, *Father's Curse* (FootHills Publishing, 2007).

"Waterslide Hero," and "The Race" appeared in the chapbook, *Real Boy Blues* (Finishing Line Press, 2013).

"At Dawn I Stare Down a Raccoon from My Back Porch," "Unfed Hunger," "The Pastor Parable," and "Born-Again Death Wish" appeared in the chapbook, *Born-Again Death Wish* (Finishing Line Press, 2015).

"Walla Walla Sweets" appeared in *WA 129: Poems Selected by Tod Marshall, State Poet Laureate 2016-2018* (Sage Hill Press, 2017).

About FutureCycle Press

FutureCycle Press is dedicated to publishing lasting English-language poetry in both print-on-demand and Kindle formats. Founded in 2007 by long-time independent editor/publishers and partners Diane Kistner and Robert S. King, the press was incorporated as a nonprofit in 2012. A number of our editors are distinguished poets and writers in their own right, and we have been actively involved in the small press movement going back to the early seventies.

Each year, we award the FutureCycle Poetry Book Prize and honorarium for the best original full-length volume of poetry we published that year. Introduced in 2013, proceeds from our Good Works projects are donated to charity. Our Selected Poems series highlights contemporary poets with a substantial body of work to their credit; with this series we strive to resurrect work that has had limited distribution and is now out of print.

We are dedicated to giving all of the authors we publish the care their work deserves, offering a catalog of the most diverse and distinguished work possible, and paying forward any earnings to fund more great books. All of our books are kept "alive" and available unless and until an author requests a title be taken out of print.

We've learned a few things about independent publishing over the years. We've also evolved a unique and resilient publishing model that allows us to focus mainly on vetting and preserving for posterity poetry collections of exceptional quality without becoming overwhelmed with bookkeeping and mailing, fundraising activities, or taxing editorial and production "bubbles." To find out more about what we are doing, come see us at futurecycle.org.

The FutureCycle Poetry Book Prize

All original, full-length poetry books published by FutureCycle Press in a given calendar year are considered for the annual FutureCycle Poetry Book Prize. This allows us to consider each submission on its own merits, outside of the context of a traditional contest. Too, the judges see the finished book, which will have benefitted from the beautiful book design and strong editorial gloss we are famous for.

The book ranked the best in judging is announced as the prize-winner in January of the subsequent year. There is no fixed monetary award; instead, the winning poet receives an honorarium of 20% of the total net royalties from all poetry books and chapbooks the press sold online in the year the winning book was published. The winner is also accorded the honor of being on the panel of judges for the next year's competition; all judges receive copies of the contending books to keep for their personal library.